I0440319

Books Catalog

Ooooo

This catalogue merely lists books. More description of the book can be seen at amazon. Each author and title are easy to search at amazon.

All these books are available at amazon.com and easy to order online both the hard copy and the kindle edition. Some other online stores, like barnes&noble, carry these books at similar prices. They charge shipping costs and other charges, except for their prime members. They accept credit cards only.

Orders may also be coursed to job_elizes@yahoo.com for FREE shipping costs. International shipping cost is subject to negotiation. Paypal.com is the quickest mode of payment.

Pdf or ebook orders may be coursed to job_elizes@yahoo.com and don't involved shipping using paypal.com payment at price level of kindle editions.

PhPeso is acceptable from Philippine customers.

Ooooo

Solo Authors List in Alphabetical Order - Authors, Book Titles and Covers

----

Alegre, Hermes - Hermes Art Gallery-1, 2012 – Album display – 40 pages
Alegre, Hermes - Hermes Art Gallery-2, 2014 – Album display – 40 pages
Amor, Gracia (Hizon) - Global Filipino Bloggers, Feb 2015 (pending)

 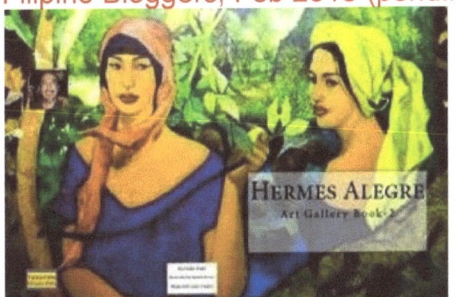 

Aquino, Virginia S. – Quiet Dignity – My Parent's Lives – 2016 – Retired CPA in California
Astillero, Emmanuel Ikan – Filipinos are Austronesians – 2018 – Anthropology issues
Astillero, Emmanuel Ikan – Man From Bailen – 2016 - Autobiography

Astrero, Rachel - Legacy (Pamana), 2012 – Short stories by OFW author
Bayobay, Jhackie Eslit - Until I Meet You, 2012 – Novel by OFW author

Bolandrina, Gretheline Ramos - Tenacious Nurse-1, 2014 – by a Filipina head-nurse in USA
Bolandrina, Gretheline Ramos - Tenacious Nurse- 2, 2015 – by same nurse
Calugay, Monette Dioquino - My Candid Musings, 2012 – OFW author in HK

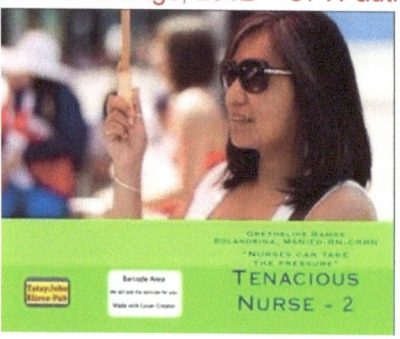

Clinton, Hilary Rodham – What Happened, 2017 – **pdf copy only – bestseller**

Cruz, Percival Campoamor - May Bagwis Ang Pag-ibig, 2010 – Prolific tagalog writer
Dalde, Paul - Lifestream Fisherman, 2014 – Retired CPA in USA, an autobiography
Dejillas, Paul, PhD. – Our Cosmic Origins – 2017 – science ands religion

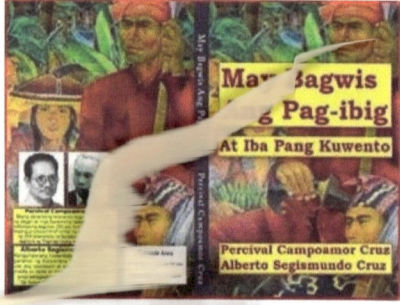
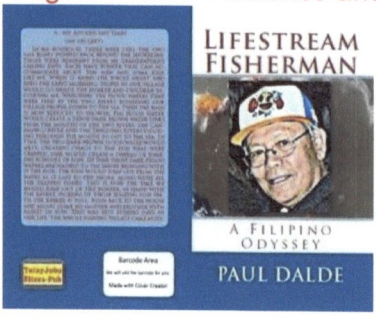

Derry, Emily Espanol - Emily Forever In Love, Poems, 2013 – Singer, poet & writer from HK
Diaz, Perry - Balitang Kutsero, 2012 – Owner, Global Balita online
Diaz, Perry – PerryScope-1 – 2017 – compilation - Columnist and blogger

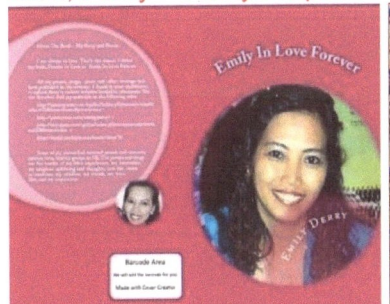
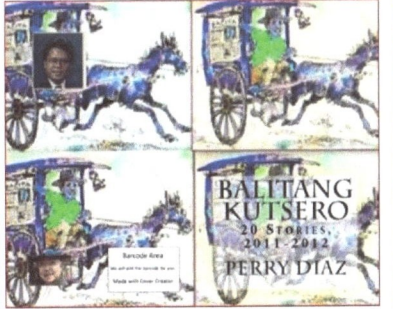

Diaz, Perry – PerryScope-2 – 2017 – compilation – Columnist/blogger
Elizes, Job Sr (Late) - Turning Points, Orig. 1968, Reprint 2009 – A novel on good manners
Elizes, Tatay Jobo - Be Considerate For Once, 2013 – behavior issues

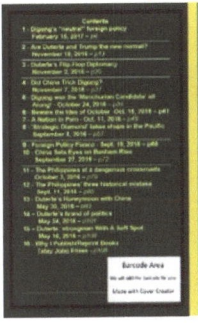
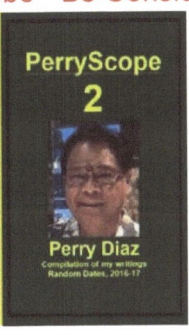
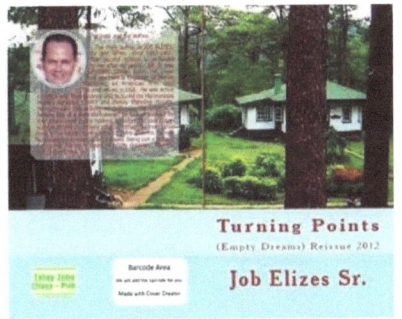
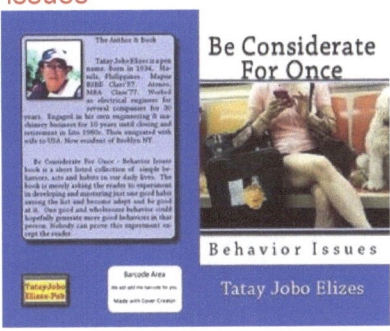

Elizes, Tatay Jobo - Piglets Unlimited, Wealth Untapped, 2009 – economic case study
Elizes, Tatay Jobo - Writings 7 Book, 2010 - My Vintage Pics (My Elizes Family) – Pictorial book
Elizes, Tatay Jobo - Our Guerrero Family, 2010 – Pictorial book

Elizes, Tatay Jobo - Jokes Collection-1, 2011 – pinoy and tagalog-english
Elizes, Tatay Jobo - Jokes Collection-2, 2013 - pinoy and taglish
Elizes, Tatay Jobo - Jokes Collection-3, 2015 - pinoy and taglish

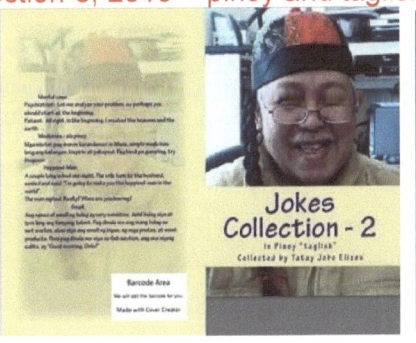
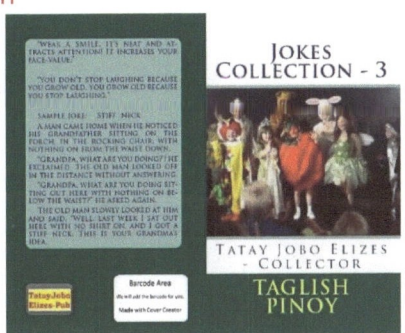

Elizes, Tatay Jobo - Fave Art 1, 2011 - Album of classic art paintings by the masters, 40pp.
Elizes, Tatay Jobo - Fave Art 2, 2011 – Album of classic art paintings by the masters, 40pp.
Elizes, Tatay Jobo - Fave Art 3, 2011 – Album of classic art paintings by the masters, 40pp.

 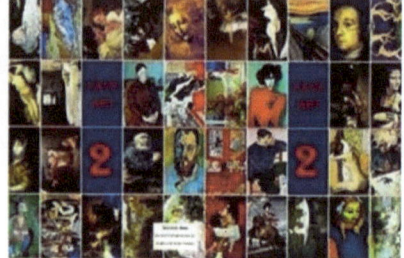 

Elizes, Tatay Jobo - Fave Art 4, 2012 - Album of selected amateur Filipino artists, 40pp.
Elizes, Tatay Jobo - My Writings Sometimes, 2013 – My own short stories collection.
Elizes, Tatay Jobo - My Kin's Family Trees, 2013 – Guerreros+Elizes+Diaz+others

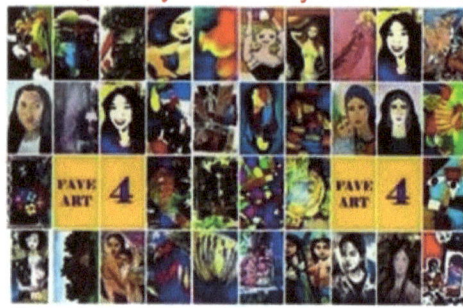 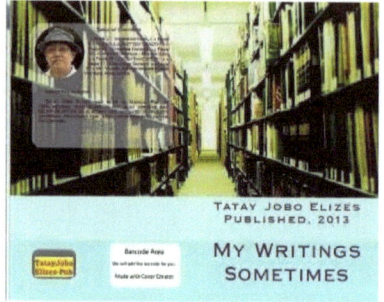 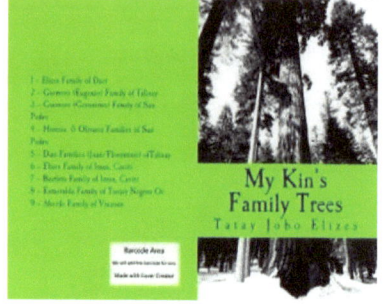

Elizes, Tatay Jobo - Rizal Family Tree, Etc.,2013 – Rizals+Vinzons+Vargas+Cuanos+Navales,etc.
Elizes, Tatay Jobo - Handy Lyrics-1, 2013 – English+Pilipino+Spanish+Christmas songs
Elizes, Tatay Jobo - Nostalgic Pics-1, (Guerreros) 2014 – Pictorial captions & descriptions

 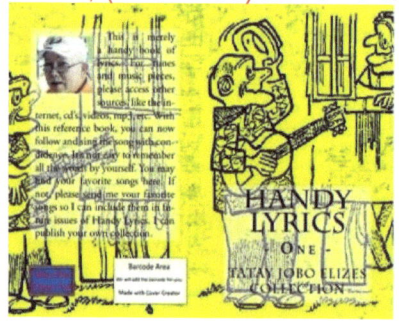 

Elizes, Tatay Jobo - Nostalgic Pics-2 (ElizesClan), 2014 – Pictorial with captions & descriptions
Elizes, Tatay Jobo - My Favorite Readings-1, 2014 – Selected Bible verses, famous speeches
Elizes, Tatay Jobo - Job & Cora Pics-1, 2014 – Color Album of my young family up to 1970s only.

 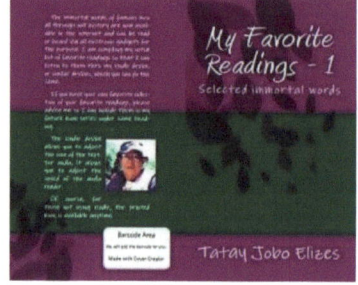 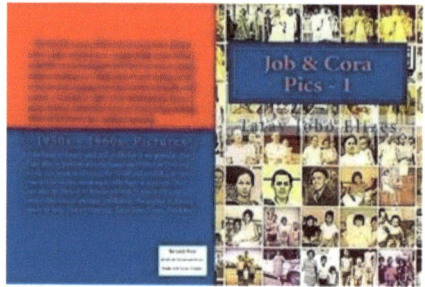

Elizes, Tatay Jobo - *Phl Via Old Pics-1, 2014 – Very old Philippine pictures collection*
Elizes, Tatay Jobo – *Fave Art-5, 2014*
Elizes, Tatay Jobo – *Fave Art-6, 2014*

 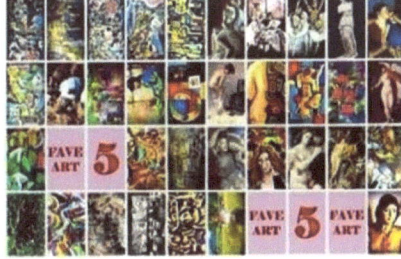 

Elizes, Tatay Jobo – Fave Art-7, 2014 – Album of art collection
Elizes, Tatay Jobo – Fave Art-8, 2014 – Album of art collection
Elizes, Tatay Jobo - Phl Via Old Pics-2, 2014 – Philiipines very old pictures

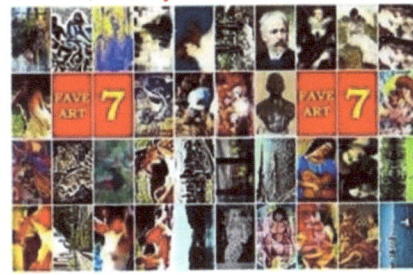 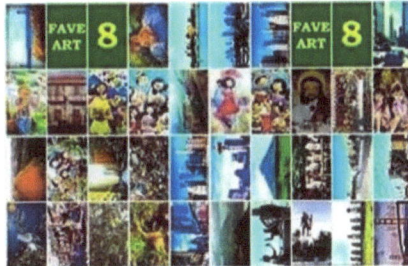 

Elizes, Tatay Jobo - Phl Via Old Pics-3, 2014 – Philippines very old pictures
Elizes, Tatay Jobo - Phil Via Old Pics-4, 2015 – Philippines very old pictures
Elizes. Tatay Jobo - Tanjay Assn, West Coast, sample Fiesta mag – their magazine copy

  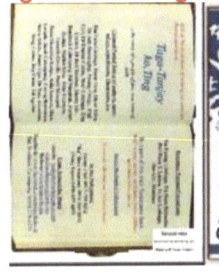 

Elizes, Tatay Jobo – Phil Via Old Pics-5, 2016 – Old pics of pesons and places
Elizes, Tatay Jobo - Tanjay Assn (USA) East – Induction Officers, Apr 2015 – Program only
Elizes, Tatay Jobo - Tanjay Assn (USA) East – Poconos, Sept 2012 – outing

  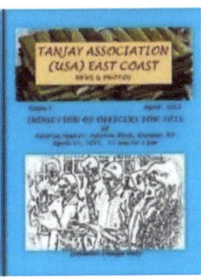  

Elizes, Tatay Jobo - Tanjay Assn (USA) East - Actual Induction Officers, Apr 2015
Elizes, Tatay Jobo - Tanjayanon Valentines Day- Feb. 2015
Elizes, Tatay Jobo - Wedding 2008 Album, Anita & Barry, May2015 – Album of pictures

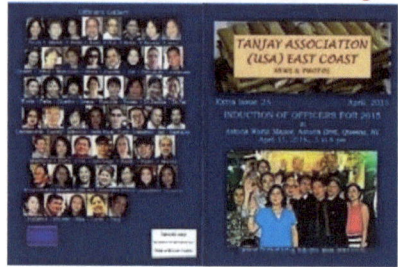   

Elizes, Tatay Jobo – Free Book – 2015 - give-away book
Elizes, Tatay Jobo Elizes – My Favorite Readings-2, About National Heroes – 2017

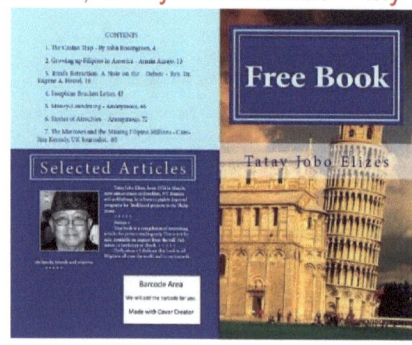 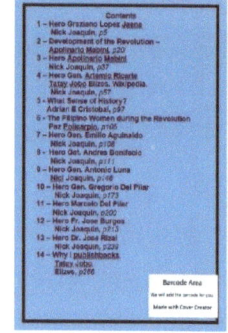 

Elizes, Tatay Jobo - Album-Arsenio & Susan Ferrer Fam.-2017
Elizes, Tatay Jobo - Portraits Album-Elizes Family Members - 2017
Elizes, Tatay Jobo - Album-Vic & Genalin + Chelsea & Ethan Soriano - 2017

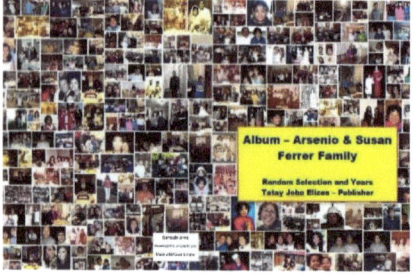  

Elizes, Tatay Jobo – Hilda E. Ramirez Album – July 2017
Elizes, Tatay Jobo – Phl Via Old Pics-6 – Old pictures of people and places
Elizes, Tatay Jobo – Phl Via Old Pics-7 – Old pictures of people and places

Elizes, Tatay Jobo – Fave Art-9 – 2017 – Classic nude art album
Elizes, Tatay Jobo – Fave Art-10 – 2017 – classic nude paintings album
Elizes, Tatay Jobo – Fave Art-11 – 2017 – Pinoy nude art album

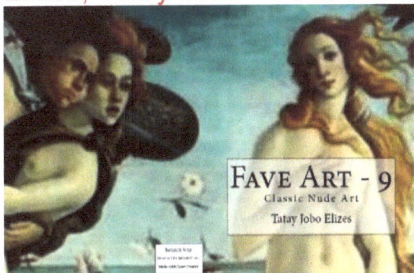 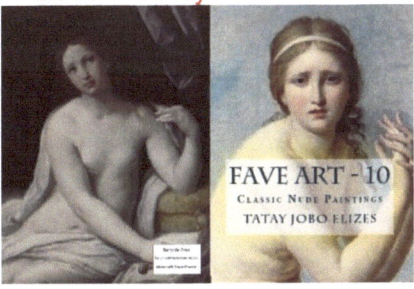 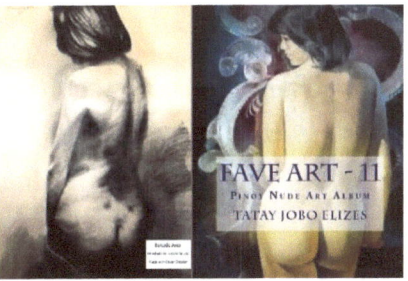

Elizes, Tatay Jobo – Fave Art-12 – 2017 – Pinoy classic and new
Elizes, Tatay Jobo – Fave Art-13 – 2017 – Classic nude art collection
Elizes, Tatay Jobo – Fave Art-14 – 2017 – Random Collection

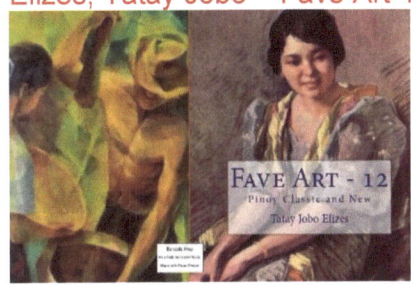 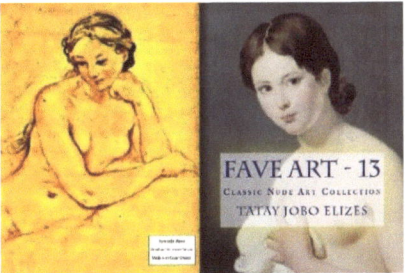 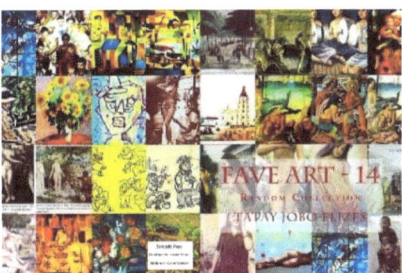

Elizes, Tatay Jobo – Fave Art-15 – My random selection
Elizes, Tatay Jobo – Fave Art-16 – Random selection – funny art
Elizes, Tatay Jobo - Fave Art-17 – Random selection

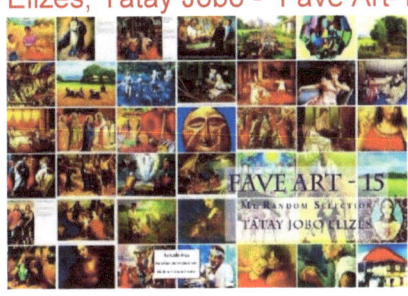  

Elizes, Tatay Jobo – Jokes Collection-4 – 2017 -
Elizes, Tatay Jobo – Jokes Collection-5 – 2017 -
Elizes, Tatay Jobo – Jokes Collection-6 – 2017 –

Elizes, Tatay Jobo – Jokes Collection-7 - 2017
Esguerra, Angelita C. - Mga Tula Ng Buhay, Poems, 2013 – Lita, c/o Phil. Embassy, WashDC
Esic, Adele J. - Ofw - Buhay Saudi, 2013 –

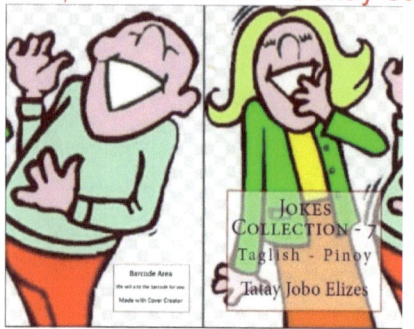  

Elizes, Tatay Jobo – Jamito Family Tree – 2012 – Listing of this Talisay Big Clan
Elizes, Tatay Jobo – Eugene Eler Yogore, 1948-2015, - Tribute Album, 2015

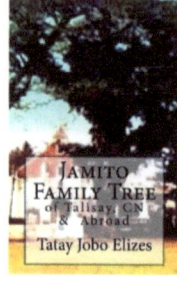 

Esmeralda, Grace - Grace Esmeralda Album, by her, 2014 – personal pictures
Gaborro, Allen –The Gaborro Reader-1 – 2010 – Online Columnist in SF,CA
Gaborro, Allen – The Gaborro Reader-2 – 2017 – Online columnist

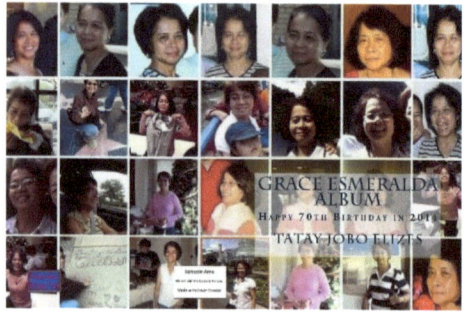   

Galang, Joeyboi - Joeyboi Galang Art, 2014 – his album of paintings
Ganibe, Joel - Gael Art Gallery, 2014 – his album of paintings
Gil, Avelina J. - Summer Idyll, 2012 – Author's age is 100 as of 2017. Retired teacher & publisher

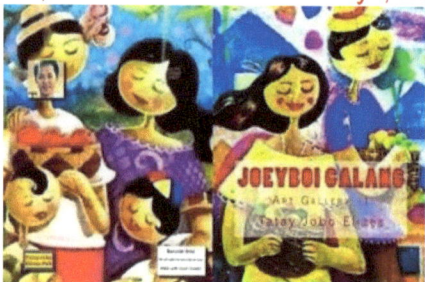 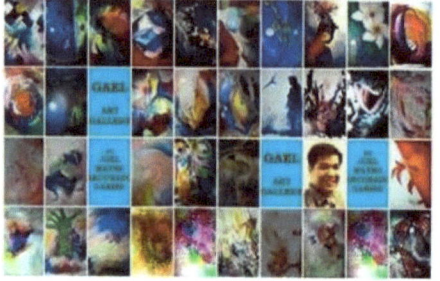 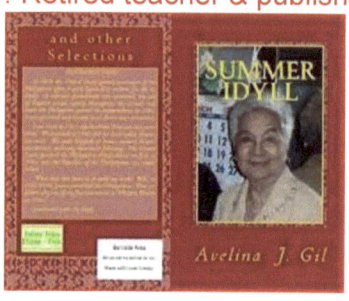

Gil, Avelina J. - Narratives Old & New, 2013 – Ma'am Avelina is 100 in 2017, still active.
Gil, Danny J. - Gerry Gil Writings, Editorials, 1972-1994 – Gerry is Danny's bro. & Avelina son.
Gil, Danny J. - Ramblings-A – 2014 – Pictorial description of people and places & travelogue

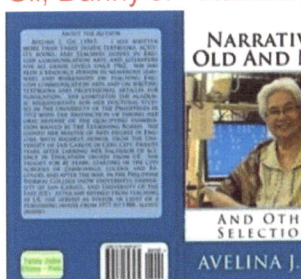 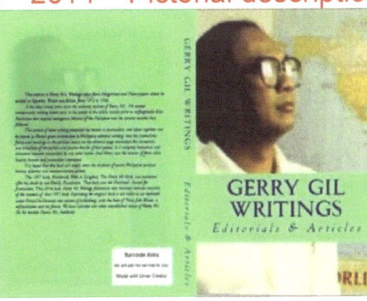 

Gil, Danny J. - Ramblings-B – 2014 - Pictorial travelogue
Gil, Danny J. - Ramblings-C – 2014 – Pictorial travelogue
Gil, Danny J. - Ramblings-D – 2014 – Pictorial travelogue

 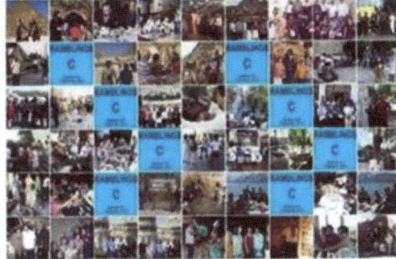 

Gil, Danny J. - Ramblings-E- 2014 – Pictorial travelogue
Gil, Danny J. - Ramblings-F, 2015 – Pictorial travelogue
Gil, Danny J. - Ramblings-G, 2016 – Pictorial travelogue

Gil, Danny J. - Ramblings-H, 2016 – Pictorial travelogue
Gil, Danny J. - Book EK, UP- ENGR 2014 Centennial, Pub.2016 –
Gil, Danny J. - Book EL, UPSCA Newsletters, Archived 2016 –

Gil, Danny J. – The 62nd Forum Lectures-1, Oct. 2016 -
Gil, Danny J. – The 62nd Forum Lectures-2, Oct. 2016 –
Gil, Danny J. – Ferrer Clan, 1824 – 2016 – Family Tree

Gil, Danny J. – 2017 University of San Carlos Souvenir Program – 2017
Goce, Irineo P. (aka KaPule2) - Letters To Matrimony, 2011
Goce, Irineo P. (aka KaPule2) - Why Blame The President, 2014

 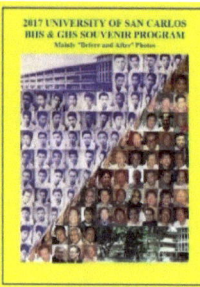   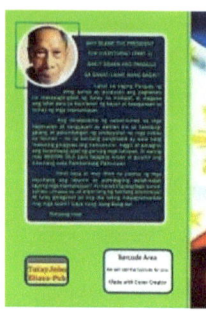 

Go-oc, Rene Boy - Rego Artworks, Re, 2014 – religious art
Gubalane, R. A. - Poor Ba Us, 2012 – social issues by prolific tagalog writer
Guerrero, Eugenio, Rev. Dr.(Late) - Ang Biblos,(1929), Reprint 2014 by Tatay Jobo Elizes

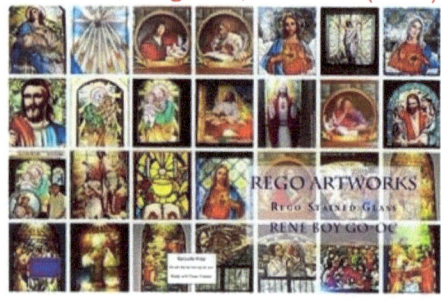  

Guiang, Bert - Reflections, 2010 – essays, opinions, stories from retired USNavy man
Henares, Larry Jr. - Make My Day-1,1993 (2013)
Henares, Larry Jr. - Make My Day-2, Nice & Nasty,1993 (2013)

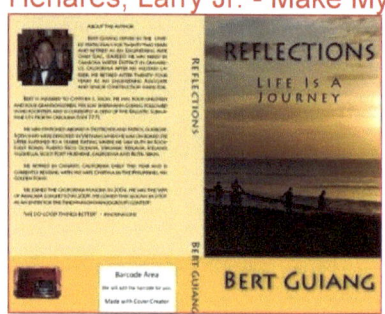 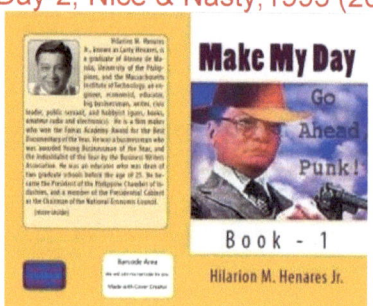 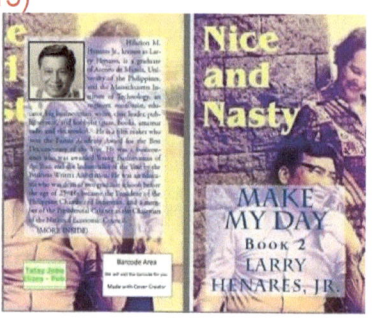

Henares, Larry Jr. - Make My Day-3, Cecilia, Love,1993 (2013)
Henares, Larry Jr. - Make My Day-4, Sweet & Sour, 1993 (2014)
Henares, Larry Jr. - Make My Day-5, Saints & Sinners,1993(2014)

 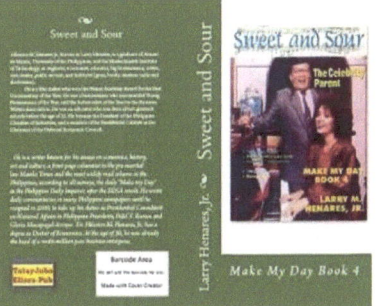 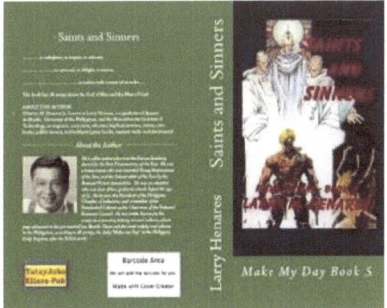

Henares, Larry Jr. - Make My Day-6, Villains & Heroes, 1993(2014)
Henares, Larry Jr. - Make My Day-7, Tough & Tender, 1993(2014)
Henares, Larry Jr. - Make My Day-8, Light & Shadow, 1993(2014)

 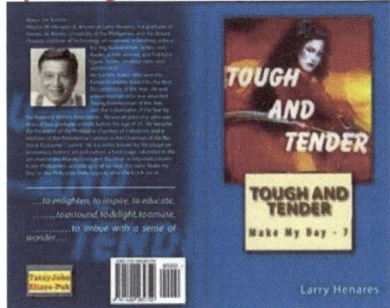 

Henares, Larry Jr. - Make My Day-9, Give & Take,1993(2014)
Henares, Larry Jr. - Make My Day-10, ToBe Or NotToBe,1993(2014)
Henares, Larry Jr - Make My Day-11, Cash & Credits, 1993(2014)

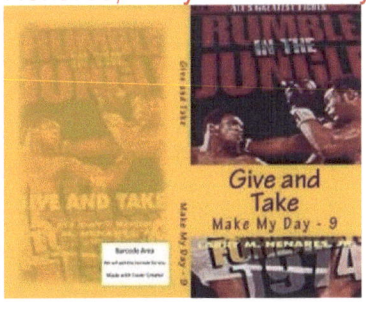  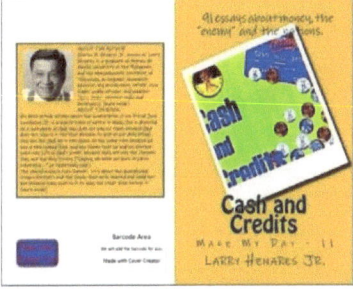

Henares, Larry Jr - Make My Day-12, Rise & Fall, 1993(2014)
Henares, Larry Jr - Make My Day-13, Swans & Swine, 1993(2014)
Henares, Larry Jr - Make My Day-14, Touch & Go, 1993(2014)

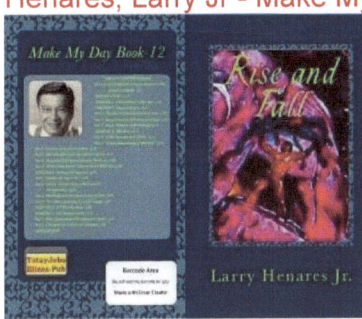 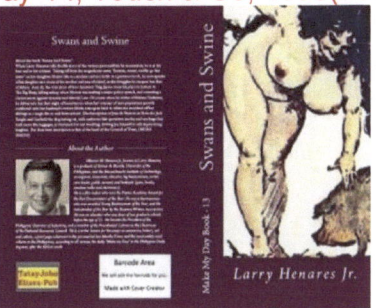 

Henares, Larry Jr - Make My Day-15, Life & Death, 2014
Henares, Larry Jr - Make My Day-16, Kiss & Bite, 2014
Henares, Larry Jr - Make My Day-17, Good & Evil, 2014

Henares, Larry Jr - Make My Day-18, Beast & Beauty, 2014
Henares, Larry Jr - Make My Day-19, Beggar & King, 2014
Henares, Larry Jr - Make My Day-20, Trash & Treasures, 2014

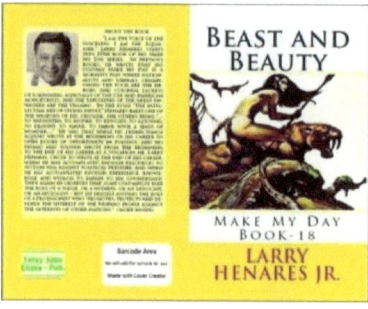  

Henares, Larry Jr - Make My Day-21, Wear & Tear, 2014
Henares, Larry Jr - Make My Day-22, Anel & Devil, 2014
Henares, Larry Jr – Make My Day-23, Pretty Ugly, 2014

Henares, Larry Jr - Salvation & Damnation, Make-24, 2014
Henares, Larry Jr - The Sinatra Songbook, 2014
Henares. Larry Jr - Hilarion G. Henares (Larry's father), Co-author, Edith Perez de Tagle, 2014

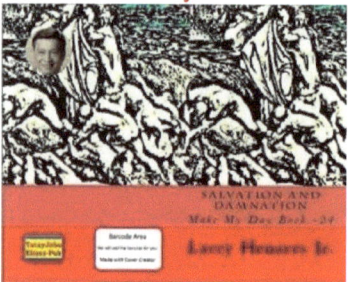 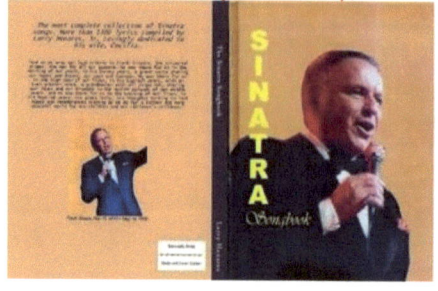 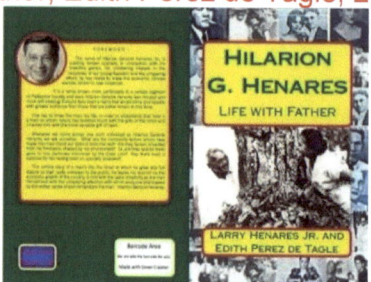

Henares, Larry Jr - The Moiving Finger Writes, 2014
Henares, Larry Jr - Don Daniel Maramba (Larry's father-in-law) w/ Edith Perez de Tagle, 2014
Henares, Larry Jr. – The Milk Wars, Apr.2017

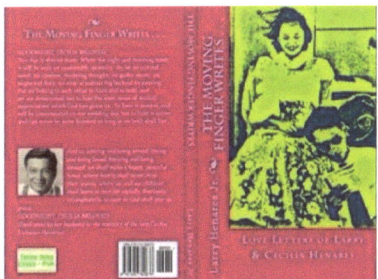  

Henares, Larry Jr – Philippine History and Destiny of the Filipino People, April 2017
Henares, Larry Jr – These Made Me Smile, July 2017
Henares, Larry Jr – With Fervor Bursning, 1960s

Henares, Larry Jr – Sun and Stars Alight, 1960s-70s
Henares, Larry Jr – Behold the Radiance, 1960s-70s
Henares, Larry Jr – Opus Dei – Pirates and Parasites, 2017

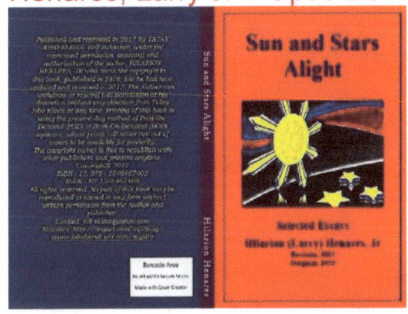 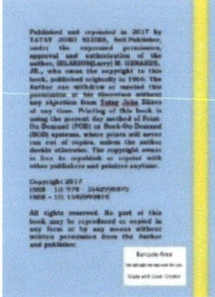 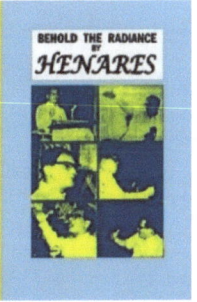 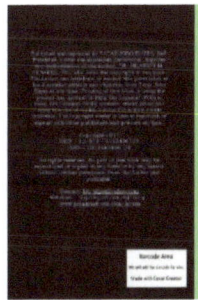 

Henares, Larry Jr – Opus Dei and the CIA, 2017
Henares, Larry Jr – The Search for Antonio Luna's Descendants, 2000
Henares, Larry Jr – Ipis Dei, Cockcroach of God, 2017

Henares, Larry Jr – Memories of the Great and the Famous, 2017
Henares, Larry Jr – The Dawn of the Great Civilizations, 2017
Jesalva, Maria Lourdes - Tickets to Life, 2012 – Teacher in Mindanao

Jimenez, Dan (Danmeljim) - Of Words I Have Found, 2015 – PMA alumnus+ Blogger
Joaquin, Sarah – Of Laughter and Tears, 2017, 2nd Ed.
Joaquin, Tony – Chita, A Memoir, 2017 – Wife's biographical sketch

 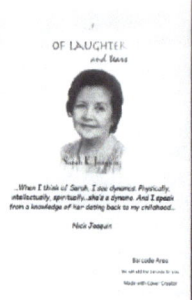  

Joaquin, Tony – Ping Joaquin, A Lifetime of Jazz Piano, (Tony's dad), 2017
Joaquin, Tony – Simple Glories, 2017 Reissue
Joaquin, Nick – The Aquinos of Tarlac, 1980s - **pdf file only**

  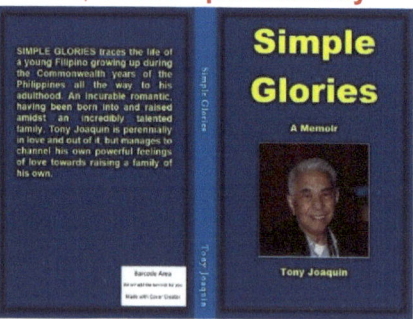 

Joaquin, Nick (Quijano de Manila) – Manila Sin City, 1950s – **pdf file only**
Joaquin, Nick (Quijano de Manila) – Language of the Street. 1960s-70s – **pdf file only**
Juan, Soledad R. (Late) - Songs I Wish You Knew, Poetry, 2011 – (Danny Gil's aunt)

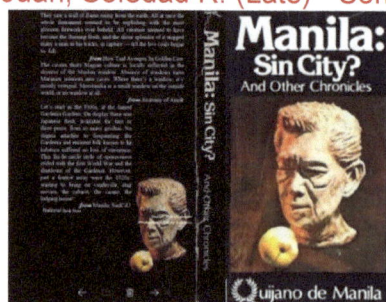  

Langseth, Marissa Torres – From Superstition to Reason – Philippine Humanists – (HAPI) Nov 2017

Latorre, Luis Esteban with Larry Henares - Magnum Opus Dei – Of God & Greed, Dec 2016

Lim, Elena – Business in the Real World (Larry friend) – June 2017

 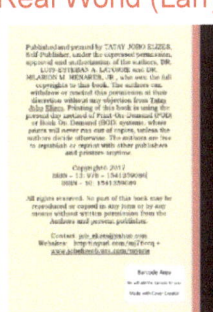  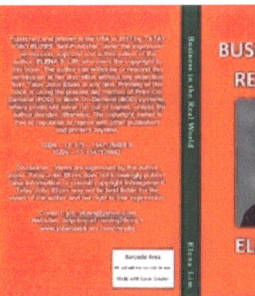 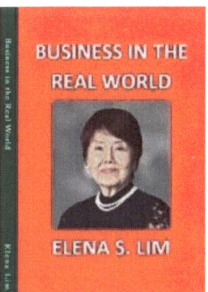

Latorre, Luis Esteban, PhD – Catechism Manual – 2016

Latorre, Luis Esteban, PhD – Guidebookb for Baptism - 2016

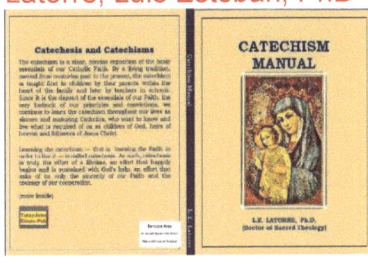 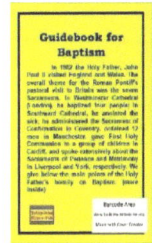 

Lichauco, Alejandro – Towards a New Economic Order & Conquest of Mass Poverty

Lichauco, Alejandro – Hunger, Corruption and Betrayal

Lichauco, Alejandro – Nationalist Economics

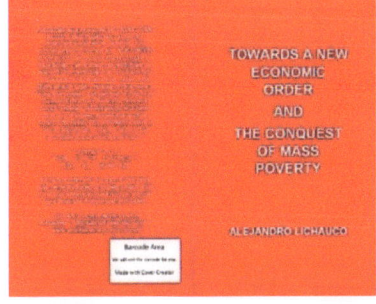 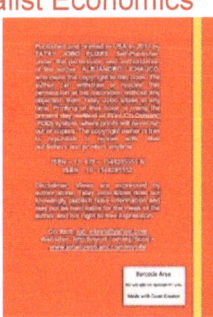  

Lim, Elena – This is My Voice (Larry's friend) – June 2017 reissue

Lim, Elena – Business in the Real World (Larry's friend) – 2017 reissue

Lopez, Ramon H. - Art Gallery-1, 2014 – his album showcase, Part 1

 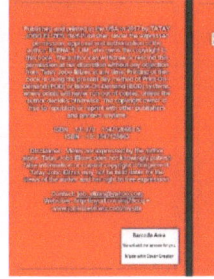  

Lopez, Ramon H. – Art Gallery-2, 2015 – Part 2
Lopez, Ramon H. – Art Gallery-3, 2017 – Part 3
Lopez, Ramon H. – Art Gallery-4, 2017 – Part 4

  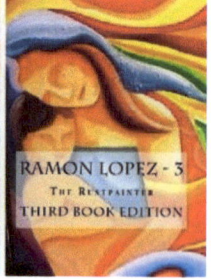 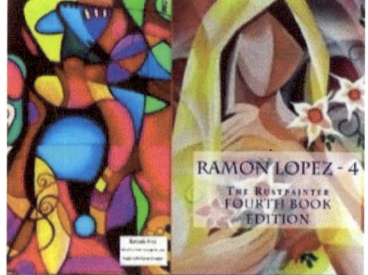

Lumba, Cesar - Out of the Misty Sea We Must, 2010 - prolific author and political activist

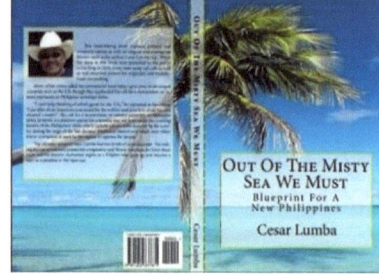

Magtolis, Lily Vidallon (Appeals Court Justice) - Not by Bread Alone, 2013 - memoirs
Manansala, Ronna - Book BQ, Art Gallery, 2014 – Paintings pictures as showcase
Manansala, Khristina Reed – Art Book-1 – 2016 - Album of Paintings as showcase

 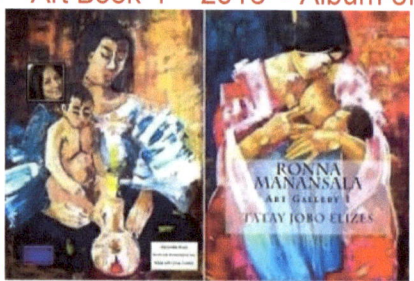 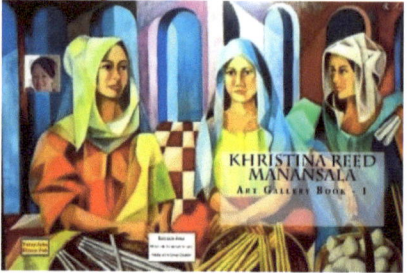

Manglapus, Raul S. – Faith in the Filipino, Reissue 2017
Manglapus, Raul S. – Land of Bondage Land of the Free, 1960s – Reissue 2017
Manglapus, Raul S. – A Pen for Democracy, 1970s – Martial Law years – Reissue 2017

   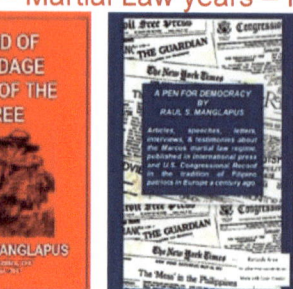 

Manapat, Ricardo (Late) – Some Are Smarter Than Others (1980s) reissue2017–**pdf file**

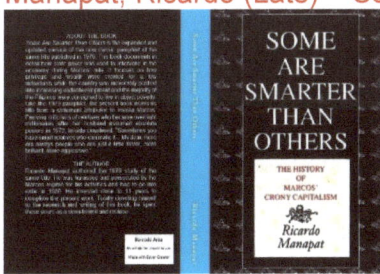

Masangcay, Nik – Artbook – 2017 – Album Display of his collection
Mijares, Primitivo - Conjugal Dictatorship of Ferdinand & Imelda Marcos, 1976, Reprint, Jan 2016
Munoz, ML - Beyond idle thoughts, 2011 – thoughtful author from a NY resident

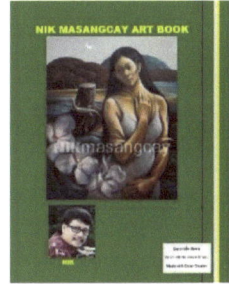 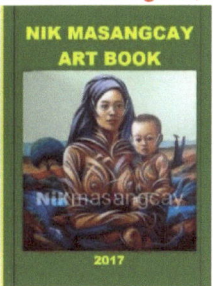 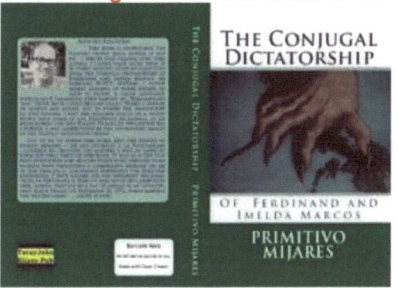 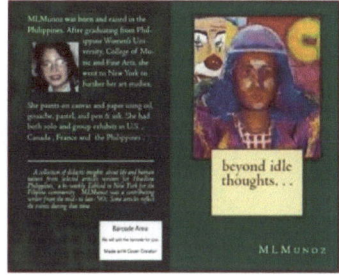

Napat, Jessica, Buhay Ofw Atbp, 2013 - experiences as OFW
Natividad, Fred – Fred Natividad Book-1 – Nov 2017 – short stories & memoirs
Ngan, Mariano - Cracks In The Armor, 2011 – Retired Silliman professor

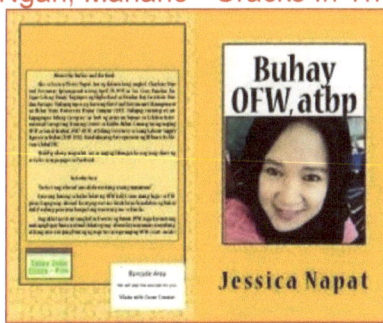 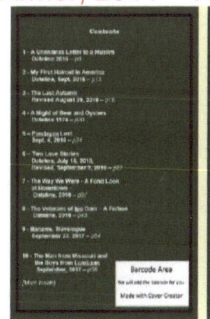 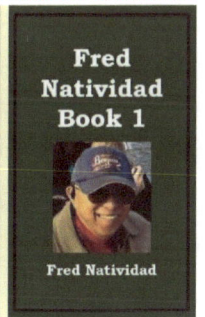 

Ompong Dilat - Ang Alamat ng Passport, 2014
Padilla, Racquel (Racz Kelly) - Tiis, Sipag At Tiyaga, 2012 – hard-working Canadian Pinay
Pineda-Faulmino, Mommy Joyce - Life Bus, 2012 – Bright writer and blogger in Phl

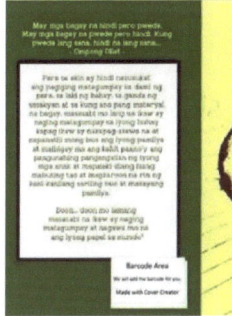   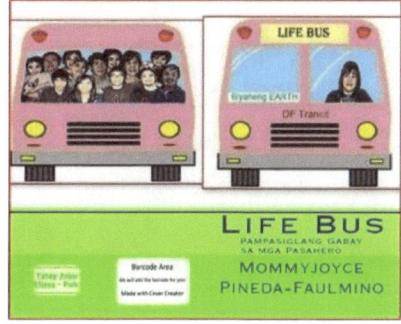

Portes, Mike (Ms) - The Dove Files, 2012 – collector's book
Portes, Mike (Ms) - Minsan May Isang Puta (replaced Dove Files) - 2014 – social & political issues
Pulmano, Eugenio, MD - Old Wine Late Bloom, 2014 – the doctor's side on life issues

  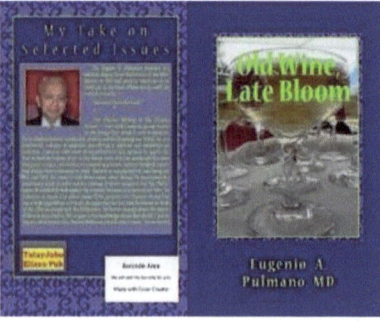

Revilla, Jovelyn Bayubay, ofw - Masaya Din, Malungkot Din, 2012 - stories
Reyes, Bobby M. - Mabuhay Writings-1, 2015 – Politics and issues
Reyes, N.M. – The God in Einstein and Zen – E=mc2 - 2017

Reynaldo, Gloria & Miguel Reyes (Late)/ReynaLdo, Gonz (Son) - Fulfilled, 2010 - memoirs
Reynaldo, Miguel Reyes (Late) c/o Reynaldo, Gonz(Speedy)(son) – Ang Jeep Ni Erap, 2016
Rigos, Rev. Cirilo A., D.D. – Rebuilding Our Broken Faith – 1970, Reissue 2017 – Sermons

 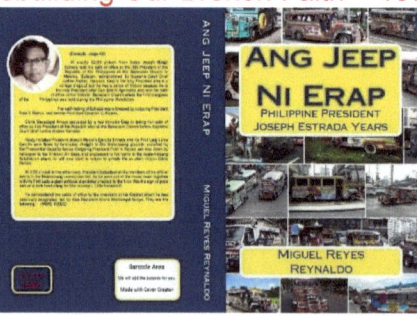 

Rigos, Rev. Cirilo A., D.D. – Living By Faith – 1992, Reissue 2017 – Sermons
Rizal, Dr. Jose – Noli Mi Tangere (Social Cancer) – **pdf copy only**
Rizal, Dr. Jose – El Filibusterismo (Reign of Greed) – **pdf copy only**

Rodis, Rodel – Book-1 – 2017 – Columnist and online blogger
Rotea, Hermie - Mr. President, 2014 – current news at that time
Saguisag, Rene (Sen.) – Saguisag Wit-1, Oct 2017 – witty words by ex-senator

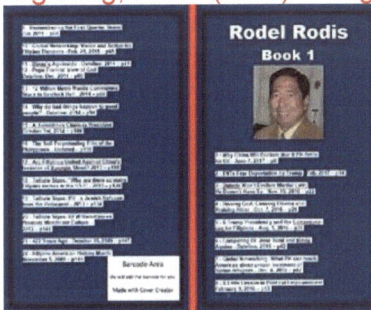 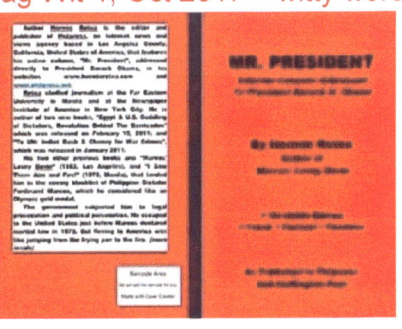  

San Juan, Erick's – Whistle Blowers-1 (2007-10), 2016 – online blogger-columnist
San Juan, Erick's – Whistle Blowers-2 (2012-13), 2016 – online blogger-columnist
San Juan, Erick's – Whistle Blowers-3 (2013-15), 2016 – online blogger-columnist

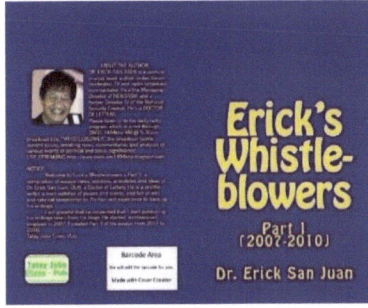  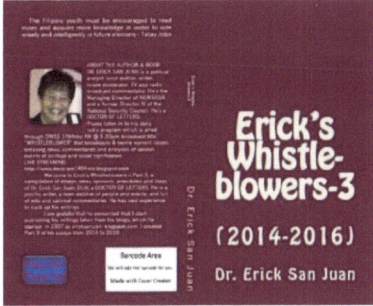

San Juan, Erick's – Whistle Blowers-4 (2015-16). 2016 – online blogger-columnist
San Juan, Erick – Raiders of the Lost Gold (Marcos Legacy Revisited), Orig.1998, Ed.2016
San Juan, Erick – Conspiracies & Controversies, Orig,1998, Ed.2016

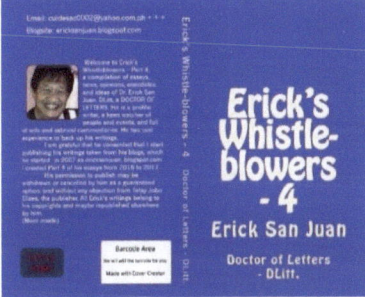   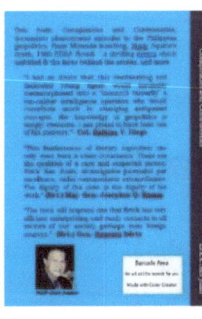 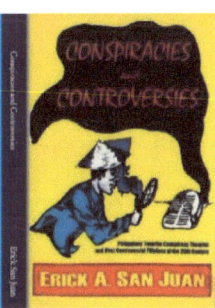

Sese, Jocelyn Cerrudo - Nursing Vignettes, 2012 – Author is nurse in NY
Stack, Phil & Fe - Stack Family Journals, 2012 - Annual records of activities
Stack, Dr. Phil - Hail to the Second Best, 2012 – tributes

 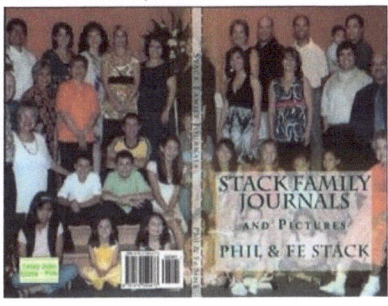  

Stack, Dr. Phil - Life's Journey, True Stories, 2014
Stack, Dr. Phil - Culture Shock, My Cuban Refugee Family, 2014
Stack, Dr. Phil - Secrets of a Romantic Man, 2014

 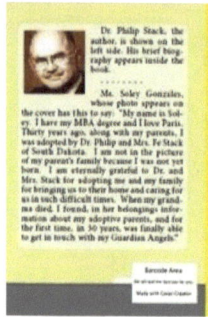  

Stack, Dr. Phil – God's Middle "O" – Nov 2017
Stack, Dr. Phil – How To Be Good – Nov 2017
Stack, Dr. Phil – A Journey Unto Peace – Oct 2017

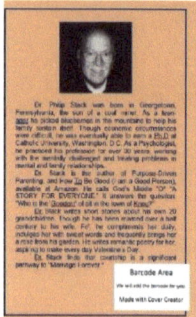  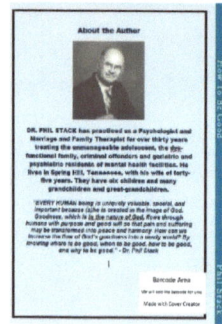  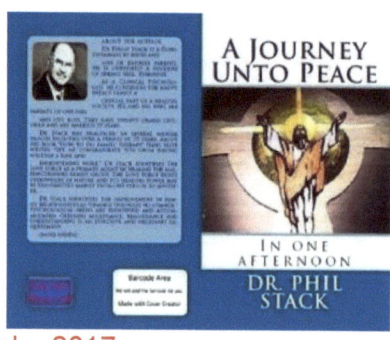

Stack, Dr. Phil – How We Raised Our Children To Serve The Lord – 2017
Stack, Dr. Phil – Being Good, A Medley of Love – similar to How to be Good - 2016
Tamayo, Argel Lucero, Ofw - Buhay At Pag-ibig, 2012 – tagalog stories

 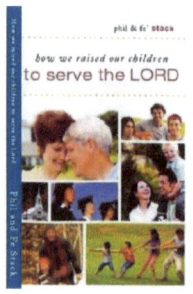  

Villanueva, Mila Aujero – The Serendipitous Cook – 2017 reissue – Filipino Cook Book
Wolff, Michael – Fire and Fury – 2017 – **pdf file only**
Wilson, Boots – Who is AKAP? – May 2017

  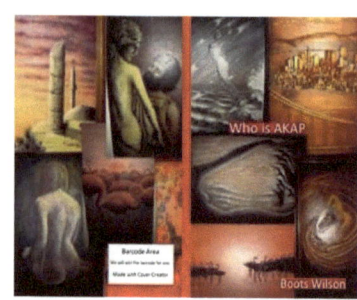

ooooo
Writings and Timeless Writings Book Series

Book Series with similar title of WRITINGS or TIMELESS WRITINGS with Serial Numbers. Each book is a compilation of several articles by different selected authors. This started in Year 2012 up to 2018 and subject to updating later.

W1 - means Writings Book 1, etc.

TW15 - means Timeless Writings Book 15, etc.

W1 + W2 + W3A

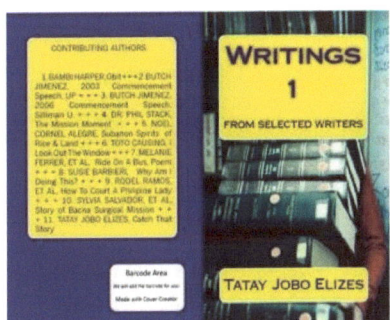  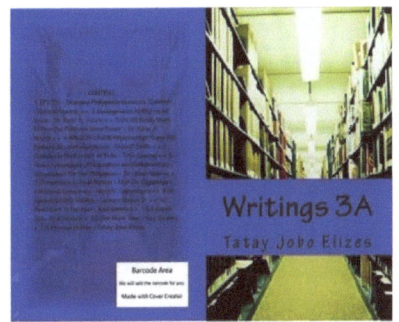

W3B + W4A + W4B

  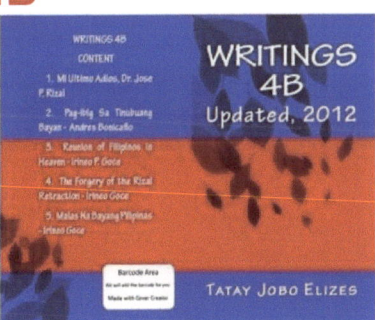

W5 + W6 + W7

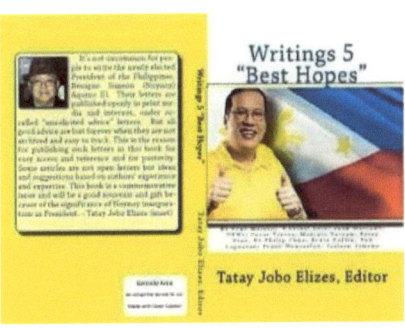  

W8 + W9 +W10

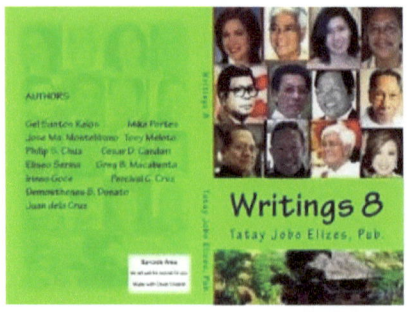 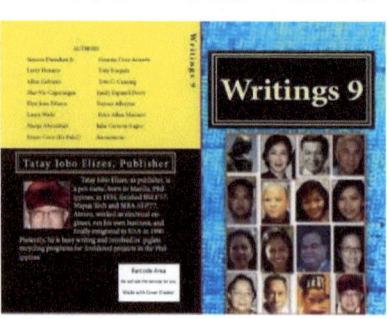 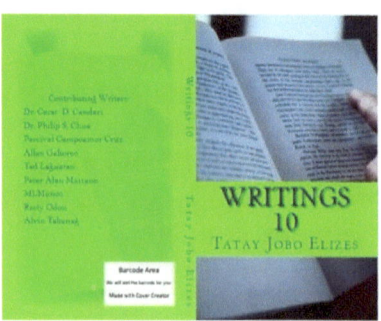

W11 + W12 + W13

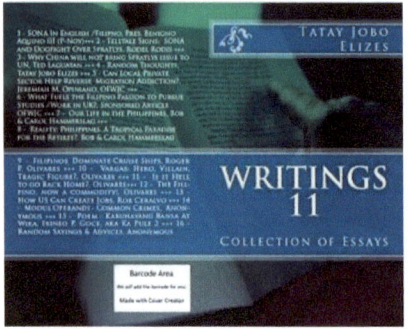  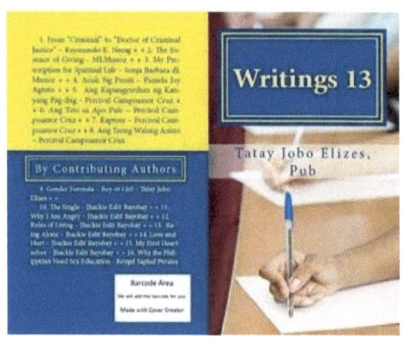

TW14 + TW15 + TW16

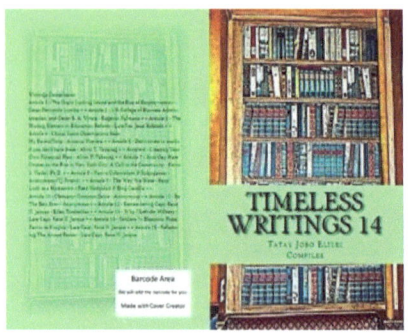  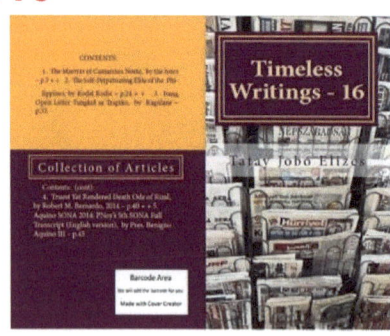

TW17 + TW18 + TW19

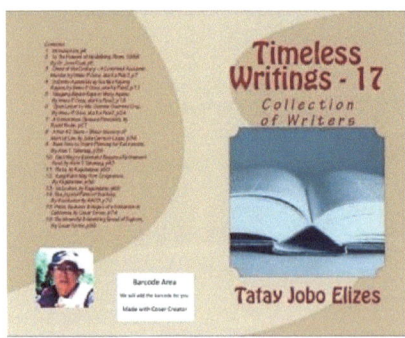   

TW20 + TW21 + TW22

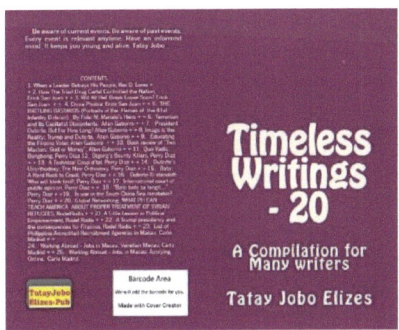 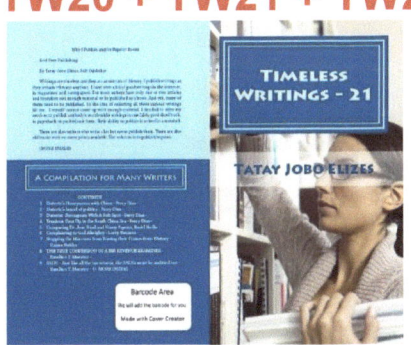 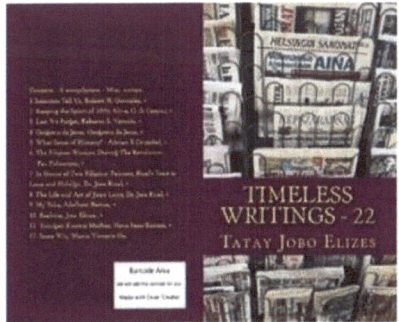

TW23 + TW24 + TW25

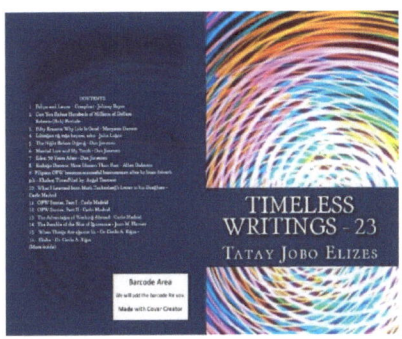  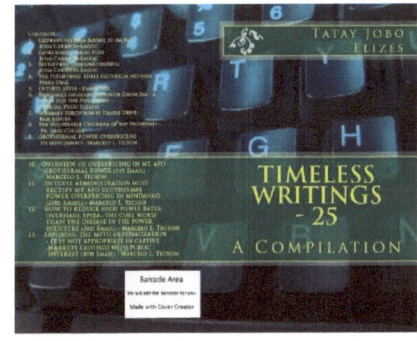

TW26 + TW27 + TW28

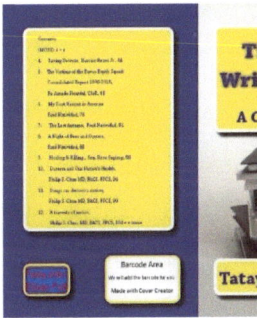   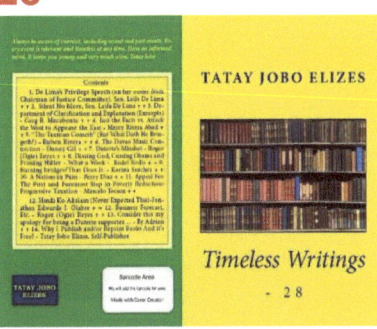

TW29 + TW30 + TW31

  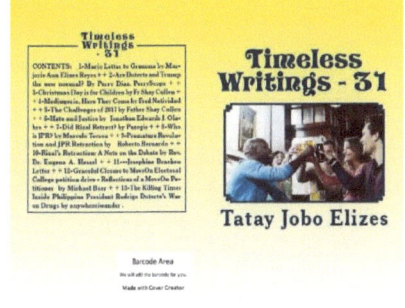

TW32 + TW33 + TW34

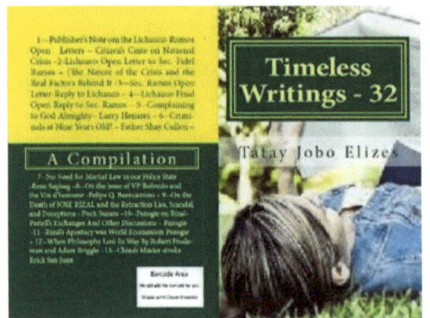 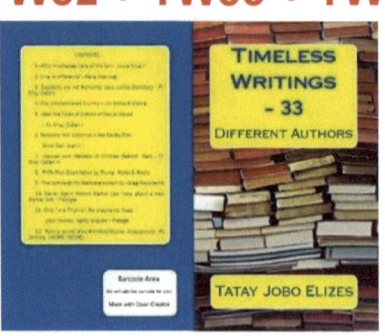 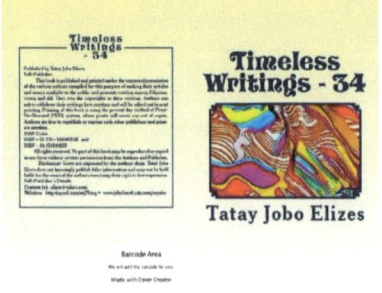

TW35 + TW36 + TW37

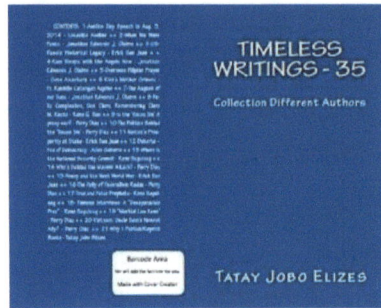 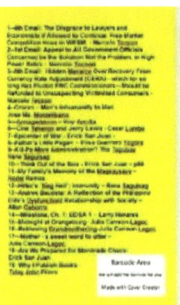  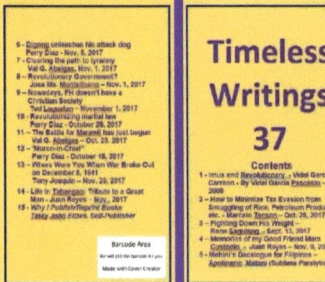

TW38

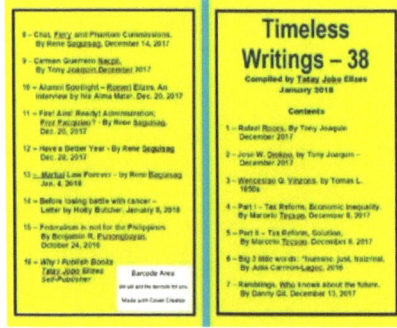

OOOOO

Roster of Articles per Book (W & TW)

Writings – 1 (W1)
1. Obit, Bambi Harper
2. Speech, UP, 2003, Butch Jimenez
3. Speech, Silliman U, 2006, Butch Jimenez
4. The Mission Moment, Dr. Phil Stack
5. Subanon Spirits of Rice & Land - Noel Cornel Alegre
6. I Look Out The Window - Atty. Toto Causing
7. Ride On A Bus, Poem, Melanie Ferrer, et al
8. Why Am I Doing This, Susie Barbieri
9. How In Court A Philippine Lady, Rode/ Ramos, et al
10. Story of Bacna Surgical Mission, Sylvia Salvador
11. Catch That Story, TatayJoboElizes

Writings-2 (W2) Book, 2012
1. There Is Hope in The Philippines, Grace Padaca
2. Pointers On Employment Abroad, Melanie Aquino
3. Without KNCHS: (Love story), Atty. Toto Causing
4. 422 Years Ago, Rodel Rodis
5. Filipino American History Month, Rodel Rodis
6. A Need Eor Reflection, Gloom, Cesar Torres
7. Did Ninoy Die for Nothing, Joey Concepcion
8. Criteria - American Institute of Philanthropy, Charity Guidelines
9. Coming Revolution In The Ballot, Cesar Lumba, 2009, A Retrospective
11. Strangers In Our Own Country, Casiano Mayor Jr.
12. The Gypsy Soul, Casiano Mayor Jr.
13. An End In Cheating, Sonny Coloma
14. Toward Culture of Giving, Not Having, Sonny Coloma
15. 100 Reasons to be Proud as Pinoys, Anonymous

Writings-3A (W3A) Book, 2012
1. EPIC25, Emerging Philippines Investors Coalition, Norman Madrid
2. Management Ability A§ An Issue, Dr. Rene B. Azurin
3. Do We Really Want To Give Our Politicos More Power, Dr. Rene B. Azurin
4. Will 2010 Fulfill Filipinos High Hopes For Better Life - Metamorphosis, Ernie D. Delfin
5. Comelec Is The Root Of All Evils, Toto Causing
6. Some Advantages of Federalism and Parliamentary Government For The Philippines, Dr. Jose Abueva
7. Sometimes A Great Nation, Mar-Vic Cagurangan
8. Great Conspiracy, Mar-Vic Cagurangan
9. Of Speech & Life's Riddles, Casiano Mayor
10. Bad Start To The Year, Rod Garcia
11. A Dinner Out, Rod Garcia
12. One More Time, Roy Gaane
13. Strange Noises, Tatay Jobo Elizes

Writings-3B (W3B) Book, 2012

1. The Reeds/Beams of Sunset in Paite/Balangging in Zambales, Ceres Busa
2. Memories of your Past, Ceres Busa
3. Blowout in the Barrio, Ceres Busa
4. Dream on Sari-sari Store Keeper, Ceres Busa
5. O Naraniag O Bulan, Ceres Busa
6. Candelaria, O Candelaria, Ceres Busa
7. Four P's ... PastiMas, Pilipig, Patupat at Panan, Ceres Busa
8. On Being Filipino American, John Reyes
9. The Monterey Peninsula, John Reyes
10. The Salaza Fiesta, John Reyes
11. Salawnkain: Filipino Proverbs, John Reyes
12. Musikero (The Musician), John Reyes
13. Did You Know (1), Bert Gujang
14. Did You Know (2), Bert Guiang
15. Did You Know (3), Bert Guiang
16. Did You Know (4), Bert Guiang
17. Did You Know (5), Bert Guiang
18. Sharing Trivia, Bert Guiang

Writings-4A (W4A) Book, 2012

1-- The State of Our Nation and Democracy In 2010: Building 'The Good Society" We Want, Dr. Jose V. Abueva
2. Assessing the Expanded Role of AFP in Nation Building, Col. Denc.ip (Dennis) Acop, Ret,
3. Assessing RP's Security Strategies, Alternative Views, Col. Dencio (Dennis) Acop, Ret.
4. The Way We Were, Fred Natividad
5. Veterans of Ipo Dam, A Fiction, Fred Natividad
6. A Plea, Miguel Reyes Reynaldo
7. International Youth Bowling, My Impressions, Marjorie Ann Elizes Reyes

Writings-4B (W4B) Book, 2012

1. Mi Ultimo Adios (My Last Farewell), Dr. Jose P. Rizal
2. Alina Paqjbiq Sa Tinubuang Bayan, Gat. Andres Bonifacio +
3. Rekonsilasiyon Dula (Reunion in Heaven), A Play, Irineo P. Ggce (KaPule2 or Leonidas P. Agbayani)
4. Forgery of Rizal Retraction, Irineo P. Goce (KaPule2 or Leonidas P. Agbayani)
5. Maikling Kasaysayan Ng Malas Na Bayang Pilipinas, Ireneo P. Goce (KaPule2 or Leonidas P. Agbayani)

Writings-5 (W5) Book - "Best Hopes" 2010, About President P-Noy

I. The Challenge of a Hundred Days: Believing that Filipinos can, Tony Meloto
II. The 2006 Ramon Magsaysay Award for Community Service, for Tony Meloto
III. Open Letter to Noynoy, F. Sionil Jose
IV. A History of Pain, Juan L. Mercado
V. An Open Letter to Noynoy, From OFWS
VI. Pursuit of Good Governance Advocacies, Marcelo Tecson
VII. A Fervent Prayer for Peace, Cesar Torres
VIII. A History of Betrayal, Perry Diaz
IX. Corona's Thorny Crown^erry Diaz
X. Dawn of a New Era, Perry Diaz
XI. Of Mice, Boys and Men, Philip S. Chua, MD

XII. A Hopeful Tomorrow - A Balikbayan Insight, Philip S. Chua, MD
XIII. Global Filipinos: A Sleeping Giant, Philip S. Chua, MD
XIV. Heart to Heart - Winds of Change, Philip S. Chua, MD
XV. Growing Old is a Privilege, Philip S. Chua, MD
XVI. Our Cruelty to Mother Earth, Philip S. Chua, MD
XVII. Advice to Grads: "Never Choose Your Heroes Lightly", Ernie Delfin
XVIII. Gawad Kalinga, A Progressive Movement, Ernie Delfin
XIX. Why a Man Must Save and Invest, Ernie Delfin
XX. Beautiful San Francisco, Pinoy Heaven, Ted Laguatan
XXI. The next President and PAMUSA, Frank Wenceslao
XXII. Philippine Budget Deficit, Frank Wenceslao
XXIII. Money Laundering: US Tools vs. Corruption, Frank Wenceslao
XXIV. Amid the Fighting, Clan Rules Maguindanao, Jaileen F. Jlmeno
XXV. Why I Publish Writings, Tatay Jobo Elizes

Writings-6 (W6) Book, 2010
I. SONA, State Of Nation Address, English, Pres. Benigno Aquino III
II. SONA, State of Nation Address, Pilipino, Pres. Benigw Aquino III
III. First 100 Days Speech, Pilipino, Pres. Benigrro Aquino III
IV. Finally, Another Ramon Magsaysay In The Making, Bert Guiang,
V. A Covenant With Our President. Tony Meloto
VI. From A Grateful Heart, A Thank You Letter, Tony Meloto
VII. The Scent of Hope For The Global Filipino, Tony Melotp
VIII. Fleshing Out The Broad Strokes, Felicito(Tong) C. Payumo
IX. In Search Of Leaders (Parti), Felicito(Tong) C. Payumo
X. In Search of Leaders (Part 2), Felicitg(Tong) C. Payumo
XI. A Conspiracy of Dunces, Cesar Lumba
XII. Only Science Can Solve Poverty, Flor Lacanilao
XIII. Education Reform Amid Scarcity, Flor Lacanilao
XIV. Highblppd: Obituaries/ Reasons, Flor Lacanilao
XV. How Money Works, Edmund Lao
XVI. State of Economy & Society, 2002, Juan Dela Cruz (Txtmania)
XVII. Global Eilipinos, Juan Dela Cruz (Txtmania)
XVIII. Understanding Poverty, Juan DelaCruz (Txtmania)
XIX. Kuyakuy, Dr. Ramon Marquez
XX. Cambodian Octopus, Joey Jamito
XXI. Inspite Of Herself, I Still Love The Philippines, Joey Jamito
XXII. Love Has Wings, Percy Campoamor Cruz
XXIII. Walk Em Kris, Rod Garcia
XXIV. Coldblooded, But Alive, Rod Garcia
XXV. It Takes A Village, Rod Garcia
XXVI. Beauty Contest, Rod Garcia
XXVII. Eight Points In Enlightening The Elites, Orion Perez Dumdum
XXVIII. Case Against "Cellphone Revolution", Sarah Raymundo

Writings-7 (W7) Book, 2010 - My Vintage Pics, Tatay Jobo
Pictorial Biography of TatayJobo Family

Writings-8 (W8) Book, 2010

I. The Church and the State: In Search of Common Ground, Gel Santos Relos
II. President Aquino: "Walanq Kaibigan, Walang Kamag-anak", Gel Santos Relos
III. What Makes Us "Pinoy", Gel Santos Relos
IV. Minsan May Isang Puta (2007), Mike Portes
V. Build Our Dream, Jose Ma. Montelibano
VI. Hope In Europe, Tony Meloto
VII. Wealth in Canada, Tony Meloto
VIII. Parenthood: A Sacred Covenant, Philip S. Chua
IX. Are We, Humans, Really Civilize? (Or, are we for the birds.), Philip S. Chua,
X. Save Our Nation, Philip S. Chua
XI. A Time To Pause, Philip S. Chua
XII. The Gawad Kalinga Virus, Philip S. Chua
XIII. A Marching Order For P-Noy, Philip S. Chua
XIV. "Bayan Ko" Bonds, Philip S. Chua
XV. P-Noy's First 99 Days, Philip S. Chua
XVI. The Practice of Quackery in the Phils, Cesar D. Candarl
XVII. Remember When? A Brief History of Old and Recent Past, Cesar Candarl
XVIII. The Philippines Before and What Now, Cesar D. Candarl
XIX. The Traffic Problems are Beyond "Wang-Wang", Cesar D. Candarl
XX. Behind The Gold, Eliseo Serina
XXI. May Angal? (Any Complaint?), Greg B. Macabenta
XXII. Pagbalik-Tanaw Sa Kapatirang Sa Pilipina, Irineo P. Goce
XXIII. Mysteries & Riddles Behind RP's Corridors Of Power. Irineo P. Goce
XXIV. Wika - Diwa Ng Lahi, O, Ang Tore gj Babel Sa Pijjpinas, Irineo P. Goce
XXV. Can There Be Peace; Is There Hope For Progress?. Irineo P. Goce
XXVI. Drama Queen, Percival Camppampr Cruz
XXVII. Ang Tulay na Kahoy, Percival Campoarnojr Cruz
XXVIII. Sa Alaala ni Maria Lorena Barros, Percival Camppamor Cruz
XXIX. Text Game or Text Gambling? Juan dela Cruz
XXX. Of Husbands and Wives, Juan dela Cruz
XXXI. It Must Be Love, Juan dela Cruz
XXXII. Elite Triad Blocking Reform, Demosthenes B. Donato

Writings-9 (W9) Book, April 2011

/. Solidarity in Literature Without Borders, Simeon Dumdum Jr
//. Macario Sakay Vindicated, Gemma Cruz Araneta
III. The Dilemma of the Last Filipino, Larry Henares
IV. Ping Joaquin, Fil. Jazz Pianist, my Father, Tony Joaquin
V. Bert Del Rosario, Inventor, Sing-Along, Tony Joaquin
VI. Xmas Article 2009, Allen Gaborro
VII. Beaches (short story), Allen Gaborro
VIII. Democracy Versus Discipline, Allen Gaborro
IX. Amend the Const. Make Jury Trial, Atty. Toto C. Causing
X. Dakdak Beach Resort in Dapitan City, Toto C. Causing
XI. So I'm Dark-skinned, Leave Me Alone, Mar-Vic Cagurangan
XII. Dig My Sexy Flip Accent, Arizona, Mar-Vic Cagurangan
XIII. A Fan Mail From Prison, Mar-Vic Cagurangan
XIV. Three Poems: a. Please Don't Let Her Know, b. I Have Memories of My own,
     c. God Has Made Someone Only For me, Emily Espanol Derry
XV. Three Love Poems: a. Some Good Things Never Last b. The Dance

c. As I Trod Upon Your Ground, Lyn Jean Felarca
XVI. My Advocacy, Naysan A. Albaytar
XVII. Feminism: The Great Paradox, Laura Wade
XVIII. A Blast From the Past, Peter Allan Mariano,
XIX. Bus. Perspective: Bldg. Your Future, Pefer Allan Mariano
XX. An Overview of Health Connections, Peter Allan Mariano
XXI. My Workspace At Home, Marge Trajeco-Aberasturi
XXII. Investing on a Home Business, Marge Trajeco-Aberesturi
XXIII. A Brighter Day for Little Jane, Julia Carreon-Lagoc
XXIV. A Consummation Devoutly to Be Wished, Julia C. Lagoc
XXV. No Birds and Beetles and Trees, Julia Carreon-Lagoc
XXVI. Ang Wika, Ang Tore Ni Babel Sa Pilipinas, Irineo Goce
XXVII. Scattered Thoughts - Anonymous

Writings-10 (W10) Book, JuJy, 2011
1. The Spratjys Are Worth Dying For, Ted Laguatan
2. Ang Siyam Na BuJjay m Felizardo Cabangban, Percival Campoamor Cruz
3. Old Man of the Mound, Percival Campoamor Cruz
4. Walang Kamag-anak Sa Pag-ibig, Percival Campoamor Cruz
5. Congo and the Philippines. Allen Gaborro
6. Divorce Jn the Philippines, Allen Gaborro
7. RH Production Bill, Allen Gaborro
8. Take the Amazing "Wow! Kay Ganda ng Pjljpinas" Challenge, Peter Alan Mariano
9. Your Thoughts, ML Munoz
10. Common Money- Mistakes OFWs Make, Alvin T. Tabanag
11. Don't Just Save, Invest!, Alvin T. Tabanag
12. MRT-3: The Daily Commute Is The Destination, Resty Odon
13. Manila: A Glorious Mismatch, A Happy Confusion, Resty Odon
14. Triptych, Resty Odon
15. The Precariousness of Being Pinoy, Resty Odon
16. Ode to My Alloy Nation, Resty Odon
17. Precious Precariousness, Resty Odon
18. Heart to Heart, Violence on Television, Philip S. Chua
19. Heart to Heart, Attitude Impacts Health, Life, Philip S. Chua
20. Heart to Heart, Are We Getting Enough Sleep, Philip S. Chua
21. Heart to Heart, Obesity: A Killer, Philip S. Chua
22. Are we the disappearing breed of professionals in this country?, Cesar D. Candarl
23. If You Dream It, Do It Retirement, Cesar D. Candarl
24. Only In America, Human Interest Story, Anonymous

Writings-11 (W11) Book, Aug 2011
1. SONA In English and Filipino, Pres. Benjgno Aquino III (P-Noy)
2. Telltale Signs: SONA and the Dogfight Over Spratlys, Rodel Rodis
3. Why China will not bring the Spratlys issue to the United Nations, Ted Lpguatan
4. Random Thoughts, On Website Demise and On Disunity, Tatay Jobo Elizes
5. Can Local Private Sector Help Reverse Philippine's Migration Addiction?,
    Jeremiah M. Opiniano
6. What Fuels the Passion of Filipinos to Pursue Studies and Work in UK?.
    Ofw Journalism Consortium
7. Our Life in the Philippines, Bob & Carol Hammersfag

8. Reality Check: the Philippines - A Tropical Paradise for the Retiree?,
    by Bob & Carol Hammersfag
9. Filipinos Dominate Cruise Ships, Roger P. Olivares
10. Vargas: Hero, Villain, Tragic Figure?. Roger P. Olivares
11. Is it Hell to go Back Home?. Roger P. Olivares
12. The Filipino, now a commodity!, Roger P. Olivares
13. How US Can Create Jobs, Rob Ceralyo
14. Modus Operandi - Common Crimes (In Metro Manila, Philippines), Anonymous
15. Poem, Kabuhayang Bansa At Wika, Irineo P. Goce (aka KaPule 2 and Leonidas Agbayani)
16. Random Sayings & Advices, Anonymous

Writings-12 (W12) Book, April 2012
1. Twenty Excuses Filipinos Use, Orion Perez Dumdum
2. One By One, The Petals Drop, Julia C. Lagoc
3. Religion & the Scientist, Honorio M. Cruz, MD
4. The Tales of the Aswang & Bangungot, Honorio M. Cruz, MD
5. Sex & Politics, Honorio M. Cruz, MD
6. Autopsy, Ben Gonzales, MD
7. Geekmocracy, Mar-Vic Cagurangari
8. Flights: Voice from the Future that Lives in the Past, Mar-VicCagurangan
9. Kaya Natin! Sanctuary, Marisa Lerias
10. The Days of Courage, Gerry Partido
11. Earth Day and the Tragedy of a Famous River, Cesar D. Candari, MD, FCAP Emeritus
12. Few Filipino-American Non-political Gething Political, Erwin De Leon
13. Filipino-American Political Invisibility And Community Organizations, Erwin De Leon
14. I'm 32 and I am still a Virgin, Joyelyn Bayubay Revilla
15. Hiding Ill-Gotten Wealth, Jobo Elizes

Writings-13 (W13) Book, July 2012
1—From "Criminal" to "Doctor" in Justice, Raymundo E. Narag
2. The Essence of Giving, ML Munoz
3. My Prescription for Spiritual Life, Sonja Barbara dL Munoz
4. Anak Ng Prosti, Pamela Joy Agtoto
5. Ang Kapanqyarihan ng Kanyang Pag-ibig, Percival Campoamor Cruz
6. Ang Tato ni Apo Pule, Percival Campoamor Cruz
7. Rapture, Percival Carnpoampr Cruz
8. Ang Taong Walang Anino, Percival Carnpoampr Cruz
9. Gender Formula - Boy or Girl, Tatay Jobo Elizes
10. The Single, Jhackje Eslit Bayobay
11. Why I Am Angry, Jhackie Eslit Bayobay,
12. Rules of Living, Jhackie Eslit Bayobay
13. Being Alone, Jhackie Eslit Bayobay
14. Love and Hurt, Jhackie Eslit Bayobay
15. My First Heart Aches, Jhackie Eslit Bayobay
16. Why the Philippines Need Sex Education, Reygel Saplad Perales

Timeless Writings-14 (TW14) 14, 2013

1. The Giant Sucking Sound and the Rise of Employponics, Cesar Fernando Lumba
2. UP, College of Bus. Admin, and Cesar E.A. Virata, Eugenio Pulmano
3. The Missing Element in Education Reform, Late Sec. Jesse Robredo
4. China: Some Observations from My Recent Trip, Antonio Nievera
5. Don't invest in stocks if you don't have these, Alvin T. Tabanag
6. Creating Your Own Financial Plan, Alvin T. Tabanag
7. Anti-Gay Hate Crimes on the Rise in New York City: A Call to the Community, Kevin L. Nadal, Ph.D.
8. Native Colonialism & Subjugation, Anonymous (TJ Friend)
9. The Way We Were - Fond Look at a Hometown, Fred Natividad & Bing Castillo
10. Obituary: Common Sense, Anonymous
11. Be The Best Ever, Anonymous
12. Remembering Capt. Rene N. Jarque, Ellen Tordesillas
13. Why I Left the Military, Late Capt. Rene N. Jarque
14. Soldiers In Elections: From Pawns to Knights, Late Capt. Rene N. Jarque
15. Reforming The Armed Forces - Late Capt. Rene N. Jarque

Timeless Writings-15 (TW15), 2014
1. Protecting the Nation's Marine Wealth in the West Philippine Sea, SC Justice Antonio T. Carpio
2. Are Filipinos United Against China's Invasion of Ayungan Shoal, Rodel Rodis
3. Telltale Signs: Why are there So Many Nurses in the US?, Rodel Rodis
4. Telltale Signs: Philippines - A Jewish Refugee from the Holocaust, Rodel Rodis
5. Telltale Signs: OFW Remittances Promote Mendicant Culture, Rodel Rodis
6. Adding Insult to Injury: UP College Named After Marcos' Prime Minister, Ted Laguatan^
7. Aguino to Nation: "This is your SONA", Pres. Benigno Aquino III
8. Why We Are Poor, A Purpose for the Middle Class, F. Sionil Jose
9. Secrets of a Romantic Man, Dr. Phil Stack
10. Totoong Buhay sa Canada, Racz Kelly
11. Small Steps to Building a Nation, Bert Armada
12. The Rising of a Nation, Bert Armada

Timeless Writings-16 (TW16), 2014
1. The Martyrs of Camarines Norte, by their Heirs
2. The Self-Perpetuating Elite of the Philippines, Rodel Rodis
3. Isang Open Letter Tungkgl sa Trapiko, Ragubalane
4. Truest Yet Rendered Death Ode of Rizal, Robert M. Bernardo,2014
5. Aquino SONA 2014: Pres. PNoy 5th Full Transcript, English

Timeless Writings-17 (TW17), 2014
1. Introduction, p4
2. To The Flowers of Heidelberg, Poem, 1886, By Dr. Jose Rizal, p5
3. Crime of the Century - A Contrived Accident - Murder, by Irineo P. Goce, aka Ka Pule2, p7
4. Si Emilio Aguinaldo ay Isa Nga Kayang Bayani, by frinep P. Goce, aka Ka Pule2, p11
5. Talaqang Bayam Kaya si Ninoy Aquino, By Irineo P. Goce, aka Ka Pule2, p18
6. Open Letter to Ms. Gemma Guerrero Cruz, By Inneo P. Goce, aka Ka Pule2, p24
7- A Sometimes Clueless President, by Rode! Rodis, p27
8. After 42 Years - Bitter Memory of Martial Law, by Julia Carreon-Julia Lagoc, p36
9. Best Time to Start Planning for Retirement, By Alvin T. Tabaniag, p39
10. Fast Way to Estimate Required Retirement Fund, by Alvin T. Tabaniag. p43
11. Pieta, by Ragubalane, p50

Timeless Writings-18 (TW18), 2014

Timeless Writings-19 (TW19), 2015

Timeless Writings-20 (TW20), 2016

Timeless Writings-21 (TW21), 201

Timeless Writings-22 (TW22), 2016

1. Scientists Tell Us, Robert H. Gonzales, p3
2. Keeping the Spirit of 1896 Alive, O. D. Corpuz, p9
3. Lest We Forget, Roberto S. Verzola, p23
4. Gregoria de Jesus, Gregoria de Jesus, p59
5. What Sense of History? - Adrian E Cristobal, p64
6. The Filipino Women During The Revolution, Paz Policarpio, p76
7. In Honor of Two Filipino Painters, Rizal's Toast to Luna and Hidalgo, Dr. Jose Rizal, p80
8. The Life and Art of Juan Luna, Dr. Jose Rizal, p86
9. My Take, Adelbert Batica, p91
10. Realities, Jose Elizes, p94
11. Youngest Known Mother, News Item/Reuters, p97
12. Some Wit, Maria Victoria Go, p102

Timeless Writings-23 (TW23), 2016

1   Felipe and Laura – Compleat – *Johnny Reyes – p5*
2   Can You Refuse Hundreds of Millions of Dollars - *Roberto (Bob) Parlade – p21*
3   Fifty Reasons Why Life Is Good – *Maryann Garson – p24*
4   Libingan ng mga bayani, atbp – *Julia Lagoc – p32*
5   The Night Before Digong – *Dan Jimenez – p36*
6   Martial Law and My Youth – *Dan Jimenez – p39*
7   Edsa: 30 Years After – *Dan Jimemez – p42*
8   Rodrigo Duterte: More Illusion Than Fact - *Allen Gaborro – p45*
9   Filipino OFW becomes successful businessman after he loses driver's job -
      KhaleejTimesFiled: *Angel Tesorero – p49*
10 What I Learned from Mark Zuckerberg's Letter to his Daughter - *Carlo Madrid – p53*
11 OFW Stories, Part I - *Carlo Madrid – p57*
12 OFW Stories, Part II - *Carlo Madrid – p61*
13 The Advantages of Working Abroad – *Carlo Madrid – p65*
14 The Parable of the Bliss of Ignorance – *Juan M. Flavier – p69*
15 When Things Are against Us – *Dr. Cirilo A. Rigos – p74*
16 Elisha - *Dr. Cirilo A. Rigos – p76*
17 The Blessings of God's Love – *Dr. Cirilo A. Rigos – p78*
18 Solomon Prays for Wisdom – *Dr. Cirilo A. Rigos – p81*
19 Let Justice Roll - *Dr. Cirilo A. Rigos – p83*
20 Apolinario Mabini's True Decalogue - *Alejandro R. Roces – p85*
21 Simple Ways of Raising Thousands of Dollars in Hours -
      Mail Order Newsletter, 1980s – p88
22 A Journey Through Life - A Poem – *Anonymous – p96*
23 Daring person, famous poem – *Anonymous – p100*
24 Do Good Anyway – famous essay – *Dr. Karl Menninger – p101*
25 Why I Publish/Reprint Books and Free Free Publishing – *Tatay Jobo Elizes– p103*

Timeless Writings (TW24), 2016

1. ZITA - Arturo B. Rotor, *4*
2. Speech - U.S. Senator Cory Booker, *13*
3. Martial law through a child's eyes, NEVER AGAIN - Jennifer Suzara-Cheng, *18*
4. TURTLE SEASON - Timothy R. Montes, *20*
5. Pandayan Lost - Fred Natividad, *30*

Timeless Writings-25 (TW25), 2016

Timeless Weitings-26 (TW26), 2016

Timeless Writings (TW30)

Timeless Writings-31 (TW31)

by anywhereiwander – *p98*

Timeless Writings-32 (TW32)

1—Publisher's Note om the Lichauco-Ramos Open Letters –
    Citizen's Committee on National Crisis – *p5*
2—Lichauco Open Letter to Sec. Fidel Ramos – *p8*
    (The Nature of the Crisis and the Real Factors Behind It + + I. House Joint
    Resolution No. 2 as a Basis for the Charge of Economic Sabotage and Treason
    + + II. The Nature of Modem Warfare as a Basis for the Charge of Treason + + III.
    Art. II, Sec. 19 of the Constitution as a Basis for the Charge of Economic Sabotage
    and Subversion of the Constitution + + The Roots of Betrayal + + What to Do:
    Towards an Alternative and Emergency Programme.)
3—Sec. Ramos Open Letter-Reply to Lichauco – *p57*
4—Lichauco Final Open Reply to Sec. Ramos – *p61*
5--Complaining to God Almighty - Larry Henares – *p66*
6--Criminals at Nine Years Old? – Father Shay Cullen – *p68*
7--No Need for Martial Law in our Police State – Rene Sagisag – *p71*
8--On the issue of VP Robredo and the Vin d'honneur - Felipe Q. Buencamino – *p75*
9--On the Death of JOSE RIZAL and the Retraction Lies, Scandal, and Deceptions –
    Poch Suzara – *p78*
10--Pazogie on Rizal-Pastell's Exchanges And Other Discussions – Pazogie – *p91*
11--Rizal's Apostacy was World Ecumenism - Pazogie – *p97*
12--When Philosophy Lost Its Way - By Robert Frodeman and Adam Briggle – *p101*
13--China's Masterstroke - Erick San Juan – *p106*

Timeless Writings-33 (TW33)

1--Why mistresses have all the fun - Louie Cruz – *p5*
2. Vive la difference! - Rene Saguisag – *p12*
3. Suspects are not Humanity, says Justice Secretary - Fr. Shay Cullen – *p21*
4. The Undiscovered Country – Jonathan Edward Olabre – *p24*
5. Hear the Cries of Victims of Sexual Abuse - Fr. Shay Cullen – *p28*
6. Tensions Will Continue in the Pacific Rim – Erick San Juan – *p32*
7. Stories and Statistics of Children Behind Bars - Fr. Shay Cullen – *p36*
8. TNTs Fear Deportation by Trump - Rodel E. Rodis – *p40*
9. The campaign for Medicare portability - Greg Macabenta – *p48*
10. Never Again Marcos Martial Law: How about a new Martial Law by PDu30? –
     Pazogie – *p54*
11. Only "n d Pilipins": For presidents: Keep your money, legally acquire – Pazogie – *p62*
12. Family secret: How Primitivo Mijares disappeared - Fe Zamora – *p64*
13. Uncle Sam or Xi Dada: A question of trust – Perry Diaz – *p69*
14. Digong's "neutral" foreign policy – Perry Diaz – *p77*
15. PREDA News - Shalom Award 2017 is given to Fr. Shay Cullen
     and Preda Foundation – *p85*
16. The Story Behind the Photograph of Rosi - Fr. Shay Cullen – *p88*
17. Lonely at the top; on moral stamina - Rene Saguisag – *p92*
18. The Fraud and Folly of Duterte's Drug War - Allen Gaborro – *p99*
19. Life is for Living - Fr. Shay Cullen – *p104*
20. The Resilience of Abused Children and Women - Fr. Shay Cullen – *p108*

Timeless Writings-34 (TW34)

1--Reaction by *Pazogie* To Jose Ma. Montelibano article, entitled "The unstoppable killings" - Mar 11, 2017 – *p5*
2--Philippine Champion of the Environment, Gina Lopez - *Fr. Shay Cullen* – *p7*
3--Child Brides- A Cover for Cultural Pedophilia? - *Fr. Shay Cullen* - 24 Mar 2017 – *p11*
4--Who Allows Cyber Child Porn in the Philippines? - *Fr. Shay Cullen* - 30 Mar 2017 – *p16*
5--The Children are the First to Die - *Fr. Shay Cullen* - 06 April 2017 – *p19*
6--Fighting for Justice - *Fr. Shay Cullen* - 20 April 2017 – *p23*
7--Long live Mother Earth! - Julia Carreon-Lagoc - April 2017 – *p27*
8--The best student speech ever by Isaiah A. Lee, U.P. Via PENMAN
      By Butch Dalisay (The Philippine Star) - July 11, 2016 – *p30*
9--Who Sexually Abused the Children- The Case of Lillian May Zimmer –
      Fr. Shay Cullen - 28 April 2017 – p35
10--War Bells Are Ringing - Erick San Juan - May 2, 2017 – *p40*
11--When the Rule of Law Fails - *Fr. Shay Cullen - 5 May 2017 - p44*
12--Hungry Children Behind Bars - *Fr. Shay Cullen - 11 May 2107- p47*
13--Trump's Geopolitical Miscalculations - Perry Diaz - May 12, 2017 – *p51*
14--The ICC Case Against Duterte - Perry Diaz - May 1, 2017 – *p59*
15--The Abuse of Children Online - *Fr. Shay Cullen - 18 May 2017 – p67*
16--Did Xi Take Trump for a Ride - Perry Diaz - May 23, 2017 – *p71*
17--Trump's 'House of Cards' - Perry Diaz - May 15, 2017 – *p79*
18--"My Family's Slave," The Unpleasant Truth - *Fr. Shay Cullen - 26 May 2017 – p88*
19--Why China Will Declare War If PH Drills for Oil - Rodel Rodis - June 7, 2017 - *p91*
20--When We Are Fully Human - *Fr. Shay Cullen - 9 June 2017 – p99*
21--Vietnam: Uncle Sam's Newest Ally? - Perry Diaz - June 14, 2017 – *p103*
22--Trump's Gunboat Diplomacy - Perry Diaz - June 7, 2017 – *p111*

Timeless Writings-25 (TW35)
1-Avelino Day Speech in Aug. 5, 2014 - Loudette Avelino – *p5*
2-When We Were Punks – Jonathan Edwards J. Olabre – *p13*
3-US-Russia Historical Legacy – Erick San Juan – *p14*
4-Kian Sleeps with the Angels Now – Jonathan Edwards J. Olabre – *p19*
5-Overseas Filipino Prayer – Gene Alcantara – *p23*
6-Kian's Mother Grieves – Fr. Ranhilio Callangan Aquino – *p24*
7-The August of our lives – Jonathan Edwards J. Olabre – *p27*
8-Feliz Cumpleaños, Don Claro, Remembering Claro M. Recto – Rene Q. Bas – *p30*
9-Is the 'Ilocos Six' A proxy war? – Perry Diaz – *p34*
10-The Politics Behind the "Ilocos Six" – Perry Diaz – *p41*
11-Nation's Prosperity at Stake – Erick San Juan – *p49*
12-Duterte – Foe of Democracy – Allen Gaborro – *p53*
13-Where is the National Security Council – Sen. Rene Saguisag - *p56*
14-Who's Behind the Marawi Attack? – Perry Diaz – *p63*
15-Fonop and the Next World War – Erick San Juan – *p71*
16-The Folly of Federalism Redux – Perry Diaz – *p75*
17-True and False Prophets – Sen. Rene Saguisag – *p83*
18- Famous Interviews: A "Desaparacido Prez" - Sen. Rene Saguisag – *p90*
19-"Martial Law Kuno" - Perry Diaz – *p95*
20-Vietnam: Uncle Sam's Newest Ally? – Perry Diaz - *p103*
21-Why I Publish/Reprint Books – Tatay Jobo Blizes – *p111*

Timeless Writings-36 (TW36)

Timeless Writings-37 (TW37)

Timeless Writings-28 (TW38)

ooooo

Why I Publish Books
By Tatay Jobo Elizes

Writings are timeless and they act as mirrors of history. I publish writings as they remain relevant anytime. I decided to offer my services to publish anybody's worthwhile writings in one fairly good sized book, in paperback. Their ability to publish is solved in a nutshell.

I am offering these services free of charge because of the availability of print-books-on-demand (POD) system nowadays. I have acquired the knowledge the hard way. I am now in a position to help publish writings of anybody. I can produce the book, but it's not entirely free of cost on my part. I merely assume the cost.

Why put your writings in a book? And not just in the internet? I recommend that writings be retained in a hard copy or in book form or printed form for posterity. The book will always be there among your collections or libraries. Not all use the internet. The internet access has its technical problems. Writings in the internet may be erased erroneously. Free storage is hard to access. Paid storage may be returned or lost.

For those looking for a publisher, especially if you have a novel or many essays, I can produce the paperback book under your own authorship at no cost. I can produce art books, family   tree books, family albums/pictorials, biographies, joke books, songhits books, travelogues, reunions, souvenir programs, in color or in black/white, etc.

ooooo

Published and updated in 2018 by Self-Publisher
Tatay Jobo Elizes
Printed in the United States of America under ISBN codes below.
ISBN-13: 978 – 1532980824 + ISBN-10: 1532980825
Book List - Buy online as paperback or kindle,
Contact: job_elizes@ yahoo.com

Website:
http://tinyurl.com/mj76ccq

ooooo